Recollections Steam Era (1950 – 1966)

-oOo-

Foreword

This book comprises some of the photographs of Mr. Henry (Harry) Rogers Jones, for many years a dispensing chemist and optician in Llandudno Junction. The majority, if not all, of the railway personnel based at the "Junction" were his one time customers at the shop and he was thus able to gain ready access to the nearby 6G shed (which was in clear view from the back of the shop) as well as frequent favours on footplates in order to further his long-held interest in railways and photography in general.

His travels to capture special steam events often took him well beyond the Welsh borders but this book concentrates largely on the North Wales scene.

Mr. Rogers Jones passed away just a week prior to the book going into print.

-oOo-

Brief Technical Note

The photographs in this book were printed from 35mm colour negatives and 6×6 black and white negatives which were rescued from dubious storage conditions by Mr Rogers Jones' son.

The colour shots were taken with a Voigtlander Vito fixed lens camera and the black and white with a Zeiss Ikonta. Flash, filters and tripods were seldom in evidence.

-oOo-

Acknowledgements

The task of Honorary Co-ordinator and Advisor to the book was generously and readily accepted by Mr. Larry Davies of Llandudno. His enthusiasm and detailed knowledge of the railway scene, not to mention his generosity of time in the preparation of this book have been incalculable.

Thanks also go to Mr. Norman Kneale of Menai Bridge for his generous and invaluable assistance with the printing of the black and white photographs.

The world's oldest named train, "The Irish Mail" inaugurated by the LNWR on the 1st August, 1848 and still in the modern timetable. During the early 1950's an unnamed Holyhead Britannia takes the "Day Mail" (08.10 a.m. ex Euston) through the Down avoiding line at Llandudno Junction. Notice how tidy the whole scene is – not a weed in sight.

The heart of North Wales railway operations was the busy complex at Llandudno Junction, seen here on a snowy 1950's morning as three steam locomotives led by a local Compound prepare to "come off shed". The yard shunter carefully makes his way to telephone the No. 2 Box Signalmen with their intended destinations.

Many of the views in this book were taken at this motive power depot, which was opened by the L.N.W.R. in April, 1899. Upon Nationalisation the shed was coded 7A, but in 1952 this was changed to 6G and this was retained until the shed closed on the 3rd October, 1966.

The passing years have seen the area portrayed in this photograph progressively cleared for redevelopment. One reminder for today's erstwhile traveller are the roadsigns on a new link road that was built on part of the old shed. They proudly proclaim, "FFORDD 6G – 6G ROAD".

A Holyhead bound express arrives at No. 3 platform at Llandudno Junction station in 1953 behind Holyhead "Royal Scot" No. 46157 "The Royal Artilleryman".

In July, 1953, Llandudno Junction shed played host to a Caledonian Railway 4-2-2 No. 123 which dated from 1886. Having been withdrawn by the LMS in 1935 she was restored to the beautiful light blue livery of the "Caley".

Her visit was for a "Royal Journeys" exhibition for Coronation Year at Llandudno Station where over 10,000 people were reported to have admired this Single wheeler alongside Queen Victoria's Coach from the Royal Train of her day.

An immaculate Manchester Longsight Royal Scot No. 46160 "Queen Victoria's Rifleman" rests at the bottom end of 6G shed in March, 1957, just before the old LNWR roof was replaced in the modernisation work that was carried out at the shed later that year.

Stranger in Camp – In 1961 English Electric built a 2,750 hp experimental Gas Turbine locomotive which was numbered GT3. It ran on a Standard Class 5MT 4-6-0 Chassis and here we see a rare colour view of this unique machine on a test train in Llandudno Junction Yard in March, 1961.

Whilst tests were relatively successful, the Authorities had decided that this form of motive power had no place in their "Brave New World" of modernisation and the locomotive was condemned in October, 1962 and subsequently scrapped at Brindle Heath, Manchester in February, 1966.

Harry Rogers Jones here records a very personal impression of British Railways in 1962. An old coach survives on a North Wales allotment. Where? Well, the reader will have guessed it is Llandudno Junction on a site that in the summer of 2000 was to be swept away for redevelopment that also took in its wake the old carriage sheds. R.I.P.

A stalwart veteran of the steam era, Driver Phil Skelly, eases Jubilee 4-6-0 No. 45688 "Polyphemus" from the coaltower onto the shed roads at 6G. It is May, 1958 and retirement was on the horizon.

Stanier Jubilee 4-6-0 No. 45586 "Mysore" stands head to head with 8F 2-8-0 No. 48046 on 6G in April, 1960.

The evening setting sun glows through the smoke stained windows of 6G shed and finds in the shadows, Royal Scot No. 46170 "British Legion" well greased and in winter storage. November, 1963.

The solid LNWR signal gantries of Chester No. 4 signalbox stand guard over Western Region County 4-6-0 No. 1003 "County of Wilts" as she reverses a rake of Stanier coaches around the triangle of lines to the west of Chester General station in April, 1958.

Behind the loco stands the former Great Western steam sheds, today, the site of a new depot for a very different era of North Wales trains, the Coradia Class 175 multiple units.

Having brought the Welsh bound "Cambrian Coast Express" into Shrewsbury from London Paddington, Castle 4-6-0 No. 7025 "Sudeley Castle" under the watchful eye of Severn Bridge Junction Signal Box makes her way towards Coleham sheds for servicing and a well earned rest. 26th April, 1958.

For very many years, the Dukedog 4-4-0's were synonymous with the Cambrian lines in North Wales and here the photographer has caught No. 9015 running fast near Criccieth in 1959. Despite spartan working conditions, Cambrian enginemen loved these little warriors, and much lamented their demise.

The famous GWR racehorse 4-4-0 No. 3440 "City of Truro" uses the turntable at Ruabon on the 26th April, 1958 having brought a Ffestiniog Railway Society Special from Salop which was taken forward to the coast by two Dukedog locomotives.

In the 1950's until the mid 1960's both the Talyllyn and Ffestiniog Societies ran Annual Special Trains to their A.G.M.'s utilising unusual motive power.

On the 19th July, 1962 a Western Pannier Tank No. 7405 rests in the "excursion" platform at Barmouth whilst on the Dolgellau shuttle turn.

Western Region Hall 4-6-0 No. 6937 "Conyngham Hall" eases a northbound Birkenhead express away from Ruabon in September 1964.

The Talyllyn Railway Preservation Society Special for its A.G.M. in Towyn prepares to leave Ruabon on the 26th September, 1964 on its journey over the Barmouth road behind Manor 4-6-0 No. 7827 "Lydham Manor" and Prairie 2-6-2T No. 4555. A fellow photographer wanders beneath Ruabon Middle Signalbox in those carefree pre-Health and Safety days.

On a sunny December day in 1964, Churchward 2-8-0 No. 3849 of Croes Newydd shed, Wrexham brings a northbound freight into Shrewsbury station. 3849 was to last a further six months in service, being condemned in June 1965 and cut up two months later at Bird's scrapyard in Bridgend, South Wales.

A rare colour view of the Liverpool Overhead Railway station at James Street with Unit No. 4 crossing the Girder overbridge in October 1956.

This fine system is now regrettably confined to memory and the pages of history but we can still see that Liverpool skyline.

An extremely rare photograph of what has probably been the only visit of a Scottish Region "Clan" Pacific to Llandudno. Undated but believed to be the summer of 1953, No. 72002 "Clan Campbell" awaits departure from Platform 2 with an up express. The fireman brings some coal forward. Note the old Virol enamel advertisement sign on the wall of Platform 1. The overall roof of the station is in fine condition, and it was a welcoming place for travellers. It is sad to see the terminus now so desolate, windswept and roofless.

A Crewe to Holyhead express climbs the "Cob" towards Conway after its stop at "the Junction". Master of the job is Holyhead's Royal Scot No. 46127 "Old Contemptibles". Summer 1953.

A school holiday picnic in the summer of 1950 is interrupted as the youngsters of five generations ago, climb the fence opposite the old bathing pool at Deganwy to wave the Blaenau train on its way behind Stanier Mogul No. 40137.

A budding trainspotter of the 50's excitedly takes in the departure of Compound 4-4-0 No. 41093 from Deganwy for Llandudno. The young girl appears less impressed.

Class 2P 4-4-0 No. 40580 heads past Deganwy's long vanished bathing pool and beach access bridge on her way back to Junction shed after a day's carriage shunting at Llandudno in August, 1957.

The deckchairs in the old Crossing Cottage have been abandoned as rain closes in from the Great Orme. Class 5 45001 heads a trainload of daytrippers back to England past Llandudno No. 1 Signalbox.

The exhaust of Rebuilt Patriot 4-6-0 No. 45535 "Sir Herbert Walker K.C.B." lingers in the cold morning air over a frosty Deganwy as she takes the 09.10 a.m. Llandudno – Euston on the first part of its journey.

An immaculate Crewe North Royal Scot No. 46134 "The Cheshire Regiment" leaves Deganwy station with a morning Llandudno to London Euston service.

The tricycle is out of favour as the young boy in the old Crossing Cottage at Maesdu, Llandudno, hides as a new six car Derby lightweight set leaves the Resort. Perhaps he preferred steam!

"Cae Mawr" carriage sidings have quite some custom in the background. Today a housing development of that name stands on the site.

The era portrayed by the photographer saw summer Saturdays with endless processions of excursion trains to the Welsh coast resorts. Here another excursion goes 'block to block' through Deganwy behind an ubiquitous Black Five.

Llandudno Junction No. 2 Signalbox with its 154 lever frame was one of the largest on the North Wales system and here it towers over Jubilee 4-6-0 No. 45601 "British Guiana" on an express passenger from Llandudno.

The 3.50 p.m. Bangor – Birmingham is about to enter the Conwy Tubular Bridge behind Jubilee No. 45556 "Nova Scotia".

The peace of a bowling match at Benarth, Conwy, on a hot summer's afternoon is momentarily disturbed as an Austerity WD 2-8-0 No. 90227 eases a Menai Bridge to Mold Junction goods train under the ramparts of Edward I's castle.

The local sheds Standard Class 4 No. 75011 wheels a Bangor express around the curve of Conwy Goods Yard just after lunch on a warm summer's day. The guards van of the local daily pick-up goods can be seen alongside the warehouse.

Stanier 2-6-4T No. 42588 emerges into daylight out of Stephenson's Tubular Bridge over the river at Conwy and takes her Bangor local past the ground frame controlling access to the town's goods yard.
42588 was at Bangor from August, 1950 to September, 1956 when she left for Bury in Lancashire.

With steam to spare, Britannia No. 70049 eases the Up Day "Irish Mail" through Conwy station.

An unrebuilt Patriot 4-6-0 No. 45503 "The Royal Leicestershire Regiment" storms through Cadnant Park Cutting at Conwy with a down Holyhead in the summer of '53. Behind the tender is a horsebox, no doubt conveying a contender in an Irish race. The telegraph poles, superbly maintained permanent way and well trimmed vegetation are indicative of the times, and indeed the pride of a generation of railway folk.

A timeless scene – the express is followed by the local all stations Llandudno Junction to Holyhead passenger hauled by Bangor's 2-6-4T No. 42617. It all seemed so 'everyday', permanent and would always be with us. However the next decade and Beeching's winds of change would sweep away most of this in their wake.

Just after 3 a.m. in the early hours of August 27th 1950, the Up "Irish Mail" from Holyhead was involved in a serious collision at Penmaenmawr, hauled by Royal Scot No. 46119 "Lancashire Fusilier". It rammed a "Crab" 2-6-0 No. 42885 that was mistakenly standing in its path. Here we see the damaged locomotives after their recovery to the engine sheds at Llandudno Junction for examination in the course of the Ministry of Transport inquiry into the accident.

"Lancashire Fusilier' was a Holyhead based engine at the time of the accident and after repair returned to Anglesey for further service. We see her here, badly in need of a clean, entering Llandudno Junction on a down Class 1 duty. She remained at Holyhead until April, 1953, going to Crewe North, returning briefly for a month in May 1954 before going south to London, Camden. She was withdrawn from service during the winter of 1963 from Edge Hill depot, Liverpool.

A wintery sun breaks through over a snow clad Llandudno Junction No. 1 Signalbox and its frozen layout. Platelayers take a rest from de-icing work as Stanier Class 5 2-6-0 No. 42976 makes a furious departure from the up avoiding loop with a Mold Junction bound train of open wagons.

Compound 4-4-0 No. 41166 of 8E Brunswick shed, Liverpool, storms out of Llandudno Junction on the Up Slow under Queens Road bridge with an eastbound passenger service. Hope the washing didn't get too dirty!

Coronation Pacific No. 46245 "City of London" in the new maroon livery of 1957 lifts off at the safety valves as she shunts the "Horse & Carriage" in Llandudno Junction yard.

The bustle of Llandudno Junction in the 1950's is recaptured in this shot of the east side of the station. A Caprotti shunts the stock of the "Palethorpes" parcels and van train as a sister Black Five No. 45348 doubleheads a standard 4 on an English bound excursion. One of the local Push-Pull sets occupies Bay 4 and across the river a train from the west approaches.

The former Brickworks chimney dominates this Junction shed scene as "Jinty" No. 47394 shunts Black Five 45254 and 2P No. 40629, a long-time native of Rhyl.

Crewe North "Scot" No. 46125 "3rd Carabinier" is turned on the Llandudno Junction turntable. Behind her stands one of the local 2P 4-4-0's, chimney covered with sacking, indicating that she was in store.

High summer in the Lledr Valley and the farmers are busy in the fields as a Stanier Class 2 has charge of three 'Carmine and Creams' on the Blaenau's.

A "Junction" driver gazes at the graceful outline of Caledonian Railway 4-2-2 No. 123 as she is prepared for display at the "Royal Journeys" Exhibition at Llandudno in July, 1953.

With the Tal-y-Cafn Distant at caution, Class 2 No. 40095 slows for the crossing and station on her way to Blaenau. A Junction engine from October, 1950 until October, 1961, she was one of a small number of locomotives that were scrapped at the Crumps Works at Connah's Quay, Flintshire, in June, 1962.

The local ganger, proud of his "tracklength" stands aside as Ivatt No. 41236 takes the mid morning Llandudno – Blaenau train along the shores of the Conwy at Tal-y-Cafn. The driver gives his colleague a friendly wave.

An ex-LMS 2-6-4 Tank No. 42156 accelerates away from Talycafn with an excursion from Betws-y-Coed returning to the coast during the summer of 1954.

A solitary cow grazes alongside the tranquil waters of the Conwy near Llanrwst as the new order on the valley line takes shape in the form of Derby built lightweight Diesel Multiple Units. They took over in 1956 and the inroad into the steam era had begun.

The scenic attractions of the Conwy Valley were seen to best advantage from the new form of traction in the mid 50's. A Derby set approaches Tal-y-Cafn.

A Camping Coach basks in the afternoon sun at Betws-y-Coed as a Llandudno service enters this busy tourist station.

With the Bay of Colwyn and Rhos-on-Sea in the background, Caprotti Black Five No. 44740 heads an afternoon eastbound express past the Llysfaen Distant signal on the climb to Penmaenrhos tunnel.

This engine was one of a batch of the Class variants which did sterling work on the coast and was at Llandudno Junction from 1949 until her withdrawal in April, 1963.

A Western Region 45XX 2-6-2 Tank engine threads the Bay at Criccieth with a two coach local passenger train from Pwllheli towards Portmadoc, in the early 1950's.

A summer haze hangs low over the Cambrian mountains as a Barmouth bound passenger and parcels train crosses the Mawddach Estuary behind a Dukedog 4-4-0 No. 9006 piloting a new BR Standard Class 2 2-6-0 No. 78002.

Ruabon Station is a hive of activity on the 26th April, 1958 as two 'Dukedogs' head south west with a Ffestiniog Railway Society Special which had been brought in from Shrewsbury by "City of Truro", seen in the back platform.

A sister Dukedog No. 9028 remarkably worked through to Rhyl over the Vale of Clwyd line from Corwen with a Sunday Schools trip on the 25th July, 1956. What a sight she must have made deep in the heartlands of the old rival LMS!

Local Caprotti Black Five No. 44739 leaves Llandudno Junction station with the morning "Manchester Club" train from Llandudno to the city of that name in October 1958. From new, this engine was a regular on this turn for many years, but on the 23rd July, 1952 was surprisingly noted entering Bath Green Park station in faraway Somerset with the "Pines Express".

Llandudno Junction shed enjoyed a long and successful association with the non standard versions of Black Fives and here we see a fitter's delight in the shape of the cylinders and Caprotti valve gear of No. 44687.

The trainspotters of the '60's will long remember the old 2P that languished on 6G, the last of her breed at the Shed. Here we see 40635 in May '63 shortly before she was towed away to the breakers yard at Cashmores, Great Bridge. She was an ex Somerset and Dorset machine of 1928 and came to the Junction in September, 1958 from Patricroft, Manchester.

A number of the old Lancashire & Yorkshire Class 27 0-6-0's saw service in North Wales both at Bangor and Rhyl. A particular favourite over the years was 52119 which worked at Bangor from 1948 to November, 1957 when she was transferred to Rhyl, surviving on the Vale of Clwyd turns until October 1962 when she was withdrawn. Upon the closure of Rhyl shed in 1963 she was stored at 6G where she is seen here shortly before her final journey to Cashmores, Great Bridge for scrapping.

Another engine that was brought to the Junction for storage after the closure of Rhyl shed in 1963 was Midland 0-6-0 No. 43618 which had been at Rhyl since April, 1958 and a regular on the Corwen Goods. She became another 1963 casualty at Great Bridge.

Sir William Stanier's masterpiece, the "Coronation" Pacifics were undoubtedly some of the most handsome locomotives ever to grace the rails of this country and whilst in their declining years they were commonplace on the North Wales coast main line, very few of them ventured onto 6G shed, their normal watering hole being Holyhead (6J).

However, in April, 1960 we see 46225 "Duchess of Gloucester" simmering in the late morning sunshine alongside the carriage shed.

Older readers will recall that at this time the model railway firm "Kitmaster" introduced a plastic 00 gauge model of this very locomotive – a collector's piece by today.

A Saturday evening in April 1960 sees Longsight ex-LMS Patriot 4-6-0 No. 45505 "The Royal Army Ordnance Corps" resting alongside the depot at 6G. Note the bricks stocked on the ground no doubt destined for fireboxes of the local resident engines.

The 12 noon parcels and empty coaching stock departure from Holyhead to Ordsall Lane, Salford, Manchester which collected surplus unbalanced rolling stock along the coast was affectionately known to railwaymen as the "Horse and Carriage". Here we see the working just arrived in the Up Avoiding at Llandudno Junction behind Princess Royal 4-6-2 No. 46204 "Princess Louise" of Edge Hill shed, Liverpool, and a crew change is about to take place. January 1961.

The "Horse & Carriage" is seen again here in June, 1964 as Coronation No. 46248 "City of Leeds" blowing off leaves the Junction on the Up Main. She was a Crewe North engine at this time and was condemned 4 months later and in November of the same year was reduced to scrap metal at Cashmores, Great Bridge, West Midlands – what a waste!

Shrouded in steam, Britannia Pacific No. 70031 "Byron" restarts a Junction bound local passenger train from Deganwy and is about to pass No. 1 Signalbox which controlled the goods yard and the dock complex of sidings. April, 1963.

Holyhead Britannia No. 70046 "Anzac" runs light engine at the west end of Llandudno Junction station prior to working an Engineers Inspection train in August, 1963.

To use a Pacific on such a mundane task was indicative of the times and, yes, the run down of steam was gathering pace.

Royal Scot No. 46155 "The Lancer" backs off 6G shed in the summer of 1963 to work Special No. 1Z81 which was to convey Sir Harold McMillan who was attending the Conservative Party Welsh Conference at Llandudno. Sir Harold had served with the Lancers himself so the use of this locomotive was particularly relevant and typical of the thoughtful railway management of the era.

46155 was a "Junction Scot" for some twelve months from September 1962 after which she moved on to Crewe North.

British Railways Standard design Class 5 4-6-0 No. 73073, a long term resident of Holyhead m.p.d., rests on 6G shed in March 1963.

The lines of a Stanier Black Five are shown to best advantage in this shot of 45327 at her home shed in Llandudno Junction in September, 1963. She had sixteen months service left despite having been a recent recipient of an overhaul.

A charter party Special (1X39) from Leeds to Llandudno on the 10th May, 1964 was worked by the then privately restored ex-LNER K4 2-6-0 No. 3442 "The Great Marquess", which is seen here on 6G shed after being serviced.

Where is he now? – A young boy puts his hands to his ears to deafen the roar of Ivatt 2-6-0 No. 43052 blowing off furiously as she awaits release from the Down Avoiding line at Llandudno Junction on the 4th May, 1963. She was on Special duty conveying preserved ex LMS Pacific No. 6203 "Princess Margaret Rose" from Crewe Works to the Butlins Holiday Camp at Penychain, near Pwllheli on the Cambrian Coast line.

The ensemble travelled via Bangor, Caernarvon, Penygroes and Afonwen. The Pacific had been purchased by Sir Billy Butlin for display at the camp and remained there until the 11th May 1975. She was subsequently restored for main line running and reappeared at the Junction in the 1990's.

43052 was not so lucky, she was condemned from Crewe South shed in December 1966 and met her end in a Sheffield breakers yard two months later.

The young boy – well – does anyone recognise himself?

A local fitter admires the Crewe restoration of 6203 as she stands alongside the LNWR weather screens of Llandudno Junction's No. 4 platform whilst en route to her new "holiday home".

A hot summer's afternoon in June, 1963 sees Britannia No. 70015 "Apollo" and Black Five No. 44780 rest at the bottom end of Junction shed.

Throughout the 1950's and early 60's the winter months always saw Llandudno Junction shed have one of its ex-LMS 4F 0-6-0's in a permanent state of readiness to work the snowplough. The 4F's were transferred away in 1964 and the following winter saw an ex-GWR interloper from Wrexham become the "snow engine".

Here we see 3208, a Collett 0-6-0 in the spring of 1965, still with the plough attached in store at the depot, having just been condemned. The brass numberplates have been removed for safe keeping and eventual sale to collectors.

In the closing months of steam, on the 21st August, 1966, the Altrincham Railway Society ran a "Holyhead and Brymbo" Special railtour along the coast. Originally to be hauled by an A4, the working actually produced A2 Pacific No. 60532 "Blue Peter" seen here from Llandudno Junction No. 2 Signal Box as she heads for Holyhead. Note the maze of lines and an eight car D.M.U. coming off the Carriage Shed.